Echoes & Epiphanies

Rakshita S

BookLeaf Publishing

India | USA | UK

Made with ❤ on the BookLeaf Publishing Platform
www.bookleafpub.in
www.bookleafpub.com

Dedication

To the dreamers who dare, the hearts that love, and the souls that wander...

This book is for those who find poetry in the little moments—the sun's warmth, the moon's magic, a friend's laughter, and the quiet whispers of love.

To everyone who believes in the beauty of life, even on its messiest days—may these words bring you joy, comfort, and a little bit of magic.

And to **"my loved ones"** your love and support turn my verses into melodies. This is for you. ♡

With a heart full of words,
Rakshita

Preface

Poetry has a way of capturing what words often fail to say. It holds within it the echoes of love, the whispers of life, and the truths we stumble upon along the way.

This book is a collection of moments—some lived, some imagined, and some merely felt in the quiet corners of the heart. Through verses woven with love, longing, hope, and reflection, I invite you to embark on a journey where emotions take shape, and life's untold stories find their voice.

Each poem in these pages is a piece of my soul, a reflection of the highs and lows, the laughter and the longing, the lessons and the dreams. Perhaps, in these words, you'll find a part of your own story too.

Thank you for letting my poetry be a part of your world. May these pages bring you comfort, inspiration, and a little bit of magic.

With love and ink,
Rakshita

Acknowledgements

"21 Poems in 21 Days" was more than just a challenge — it was a journey of discipline, emotion, and self-discovery. Every day brought a blank page, and every blank page invited a truth to unfold.

I offer my deepest gratitude to the quiet moments that whispered inspiration, and the storms that stirred thoughts deeper than words. This book would not exist without the power of time, the pulse of feeling, and the will to keep writing, even on days when the ink felt heavy.

To those who believed in me, even when I doubted myself — thank you.

To every poet who came before me and to every reader who holds this book now — thank you for giving poetry a place in the world.

And most importantly, to the version of myself who chose to begin — this is your triumph.

With gratitude,
Rakshita S

1.. Me, You and All

Something meant to be unconditional
Where every time seems to be minimal

Whose aura evolves me, you and all
Whose essence brightens, now and then
Whose desire is to bless me, you and all
Whose harmony lightens, now and then

Could be the touch, memory or dream
Where one can go insane, calm or even scream
Could be soul-mates, twin flames, a pet, a parent, a child
or a sibling
Where one can blindly defy every failing and ceiling

Something which strengthens me, you and all
With that, one will feel like the king of the world of all
minds
Sometimes weakens me, you and all
With that, one will feel like losing all at once in the race
of mankind

The vigour in heart, the sparkle in eyes
The calmness in mind is needed by you, me and all
Believe in someone who gifts their time, in the era of
'time flies'
As it is most precious for you, me and all

We have it all
We are nothing without it at all
One can find it in me, you and all
Oh, you guessed it right, it is LOVE beyond all

2. Plan Of Action

You are a person of your own words
Keep them monitored with mind swords

Let it take time
Let it be slow
But don't just go with the flow
Follow your heart, then
Every action of yours will make you glow

Not necessary to have a Plan Of Action
ready on the plate
Rather, let your heart follow your passion

But But But
Never promise someone without a Plan of Action
Cut Cut Cut
The ropes of rules and ethics, if you promised to take the
Action

If it has your heart and devotion
You will have the Plan of Action

So, take a pause
Give it a thought
Is that what you always want

So, take a deep breath
Give it a shot
Is that what you always loved

So, take a glance around you
Be it a glossy cohort
Is that what you always dreamt of

And you got an action in plan
without jotting it down
Since it came directly from you heart deep down

3. Dream for yourself

Be the writer of your dreams
Never hold to anyone for your desires

Be the director of your life at every mile
Say Light, Camera & Action, for your every step, now
and then, while

Be your musician
Just hum the melody of your choices

Be your lyricist
Create every verse and stanza full of your strong-willed
fist

Be your screenwriter
Let every move play on your demand, it can be either
lighter or fighter

Be the gaffer of every circuit you choose to follow
Let the current sparkle your every cell, and understand

what is solid and what is hollow

Always chase your dreams
Without indulgence of any collateral creams

Never convince yourself to be part of someone else's
dreams
Because in the world of today, no one will hold on to
your dreams

We are the reason for every event in our lives
Never tremble upon what is vain and what is gain, in
strife

4. A Moment

A moment is a picture clicked
Leaves a snap in your heart

A moment can be so powerful
A moment can be forgetful

Its not the moment
It' s how much US in the moment

The morning ray
The moment we pray

The noon sleep
The moment we work hard to upkeep

The evening calmness
The moment for thankfulness

The night set
The moment we met

The winters so chill
The moment which gets us thrill

The summers so hot
The moment to get on a oceanic thought

The rains full of love
The moment to swim like a dove

The autumn so dazzling
The moment for admiring

A moment can be full of you with all
A moment can be full of you in all

A moment can be full of all in you
A moment can be full of all of you

A moment is like a pearl
Let its shell be prideful

A moment is like a dew
Let it shine as it is new

A moment can be strong
A moment can be weak

Lets cherish all the moments
Hearty smile in all moments

Don't let their count limited to few
Every time make them ecstatically new

5. Confidence A success key

Staring a cloud nine
With lots of hope and shine
Among the noise of chirping birds
There will be some cuckoo, crow and humming bird

Try to hear to voice which resonates with your heart
Follow the one which lead you to your definite dart

The dust, the dew, the moist, the light, the rays
Let them be your serving trays

The cold, the hot, the temperate zone
Let them be your winning stone

No one can stop you
No one can command on you
Be your own commander,
Bear all the hurdles like, you are your own endorser

Sometimes a ray may disguise you

Until when it can astray you
You will rise
You will shine

Confidence is the only key to come forward
from a broken bridge with cherishing smile.
Confidence is the only weapon which
let you to tear off the chains of snag mile by mile.

So, look forward and move ahead
The nightingale is chanting your success story
Check arounds and walk ahead
Lets walk on red carpet with a never ending story

6. Dreams, Fear and Reality

Standing amidst the crowd
Yet picturing the portrait of dreams
The encompassing sound which is quiet but loud
Behaving at your best with bounded streams

Taking a breath for who are around
Inhaling for heart which is inaudibly pound
Consistently living in the parallel world
Trying to stay at conventional yet swirled

These fears are not letting us to have in the present
moment
These fears are causing to life a two-way life
How can we allow something which is taking away the
conscious mind
How can we let this fear to overpower and shadow the,
what we can find

Lets manifest the power of smile and good hope and best
things

Lets be thankful for what we have, be courageous for
what we did
Make peace with your thoughts, welcome the happiness
in every lot
Chant whatever gives you calmness, take a deep breath
and roar to all timidness

You are sky without any limits.
You are the land with humbleness and self-
efficaciousness.
You are the air without any perimeter .
With all this, you are as-like-as water which pacifies
everything.
Be YOU everywhere, you will be happy and calm.

7. Miss My Younger Self

I miss being my younger self
The fearlessness, the ignorance
the innocence, the naivety
It was a bundle of kids growing up to act like smart kids

Learning to meet people, greet people, and bond with
people
Yet blubbering on the dumb act of blind trust
Learning to stand on my own, a new city, new food and
a new phase
Yet enjoying now and then, without a glitch of what can
go wrong by then

Was able to make lifetime memories
With the people who taught me, so many stories
Ohh, I miss those people.

Managing the finances, groceries and the gossips all
together
Without a wrinkle on the forehead and a word of 'stress'

in the dictionary of life
With few responsibilities, mainly of myself
Yet taking every step like a grown-up kid with
awareness in mind and butterflies in the heart.

Was able to learn many life notes
Handling the situations around, along with amazing
people, with their anecdotes
Ohh, I miss those days

Stepping out of the comfort zone, trying out new things,
without a single thought of consequences.
Loving the vibe around and fighting all odds
With the zeal in sparkling eyes and the gusto of all the
odd.

Always be thankful for the learnings, memories and
pictures that I had
Will keep cherishing the days I had

8. Be only the best human

People have illustrated this Life is as a race,
Be it a career, education or stream you face.

Yes it is true to some extent
But only if you treat it like insta post with famous
content

Apart from it, there are relations which people like to
chase
And have made their lives like a corn maze

Everyone wants to be a good son, a good daughter, a
good spouse and so on
Why to feel this pressure, with the people who are our
only unplanned well-wishers.

Why to be always on a scale of best to worst or good to
bad,
that too in relations which have made you this lad

Try to be a good human only
Just be honest with your soul fully

Why to doubt every choice and voice
Doubting yourself and craving for all rejoice

Humanity is the best gesture, be it your air drop
And you will land up in a runway of cream of the crop

9. Someone to pour your heart

Be glad if you have someone to speak your heart out
No filters, no mediators, no mistrust, no fabrication

Be glad if you have someone with whom you can spend
hours without speaking a word
No expressions, no noise, no arguments, no questions
asked

Be glad if you have someone to talk to, even after
months, with same excitement every time
No simulation, no stimulation, no judgement, no fake
answers to give

And you are an adult and don't have that one person
Don't lose your heart
You were never meant for those

Be thankful for the aura you have, which does not
resonate easily or naively

No false promises, no humbuggery, no fear, no strings
attached

Be glad for the strong and brave mind & heart you carry
Always attentive, always wise, always sharp, always
humble

Be glad for the strength you show with chaos in heart
and chirping in mind
Always brave, always helping, always faithful, always a
WINNER

10. Perspective

It is never right or wrong
It is always the point of view of someone

What can be right for me, could be wrong for you
What can be right for you, could be wrong for me

We may never know who is sailing across which river
And they have a different view, which makes you shiver

We may never know what someone is dealing with
And they have a different opinion of sight to stand
strong with

Everyone has varying upbringing, nature and sulook
And yes they have a different outlook

That's why Everyone is different,
Which sometimes, appear to others as indifferent

Then why to judge, even after knowing the root notion

And avoid smudging your relationship, bond and
emotion

Never self-doubt on your opinion, put forth your
thought
Respecting the ideas of others without any cut-short

It takes patience ride to absorb perspectives from all
angles
But the destination you land up is the ultimate snuggle
mingle

If you have the courage to lend your hand,
and help someone out of the difficult times
Do it without any expectation and without judging from
any end
and learn to accept their perspective to strengthen the
bond ties

Let your perspective be alive
And Let the perspective of others thrive

11. The Choice

Taking a decision has always been a multiple-choice
question
with an allowed answer more than one,
Every choice makes it difficult to have one

Destiny is like the needle of life
While the thread plays a 'Choice'
Dare to raise your voice
Your willpower will be shortened to thrice

Yes, we do have multiple threads,
like heartfelt wishes, family expectations, societal norms
Trying to overshadow the wish, like a silk out of worms

Each wire of satire waits to enter the needle
Catching the bit of each of them, a wounded wire makes
a way through it
Oh, the wounded one now has to tie the ends,
Already battling, but ending up in the battle of public
norms

Why does it happen to people who are kind and naive,
mostly
Why do the external factors trigger the reactions,
ghostly
Keeping quiet and smiling loud
making the heart calm down, in every pound

Accepting the blurry view with a spectacle of rules and
ethics
Forgetting our choice and caring about others' picks

Can't they try to answer only one of their choice?
With no pressure of selecting other optimal answers
which are fierce and lost all their rejoice
Life is a gift, please keep it simple and care for it
With thread of choice & with needle in your hand.

12. What we think we are

We should be best for ourself then for others
Never let filter of someone for us to bother

Always be the best version in your eyes, first
Then try to light up your image thirst

Be truthful with your heart and mind
Be a brave soul yet kind

Drop the idea of people thinking about you
Because they aren't really
Its the hype, you give to yourself virtually

Be best, just within yourself
You will attract the best and put your mind at rest

We do see, what we want to see
And become biased while judging ourselves from
someone else's mind

People will say something, people will hide something
some will say, what you want to hear
some will say, what they want to tell

Be ready to listen all the thoughts
because we live in a society of many shots and bots
But never let any of them to enter to brain and reach
heart
This noise should never let you loose any of your goal-
chart

Let them be the king of their world
And Be the Ruler of your world

13. Keep It Simple

The rising sun and the wavy ocean
All are bounded in the laws of nature
Have they ever tried to go out of their allocated brochure
!!

Yeah, they roar sometimes,
Someday Sun takes a break and skips light for us
Someday ocean soars high, forgetting about low tides
And they are back to normal,
Keeping it simple

The bloomy flower and the buzzing bumblebee
All are endeavouring rules of this cosmos
Have they ever switched to other ross-toss !!

Yeah, sometimes they mellow down
The flower withers and
The bumblebee takes some rest
And they are back to normal

Keeping it simple

Homo sapiens are complicating the things
And complaining 'Why this, why that'
Can't they accept the reality and
Keep it Simple

Nature is the biggest mentor
Absorb every teaching of our earth
Feel the happy butterflies gurgling all around your heart
Please Keep It Simple

14. The Princess

She was little girl always
A gullible one with blind trust
You made her believe that she is the Princess.

She was a simple girl since childhood
An insanely loving one, hoping to get some
You made her believe that she is Precious

She was a happy crazy girl,
Lending a shoulder even to the ones, who were never
with her
You made her believe that she is Special

She was a timid girl,
Scared of the people, society and ethics of her own
You made her believe that she is like a Lion

She was mediocre grade person
Lacking the confidence and trying to fit in the

competitive world
You made her believe that she is the Best of all

Instead of treating her like a little precious princess
And letting her dream the world she never owns
You could have told her the reality and asked her to be a
Woman

Instead to dismantling her trust
And shattering her to believe anywhere again
You could have told her the truth and asked her to be the
independent one

If a girl trust you blindly, madly and foolishly
She is living like a Princess, only your Princess
But you should have asked her to be the Queen
Not so gullible but intelligent
Not so faint-hearted but unshaken

15. That's all I want

When I am chasing my dreams, working hard - day &
night
Running round the clock, to reach goal of ambitious
height
A little support and words of motivation
That's all I want

When I am having a teary-eye, with emotional turmoil
Thinking all about the way move out of that anxious
nervy coil
A small talk and a tight hug
That's all I want

When I am having a cheerful time, with all my loved
ones around
Living on the dream land, wishing to have such good
time every round
A big smile and a happy eyes

That's all I want

When I am sitting alone, overthinking the situation
Throttling over the hypothetical - yes-no-games
A heart to calm me down and a gesture to make me
smile
That's all I want

When I am wishing to have someone to talk to; When I
have, a lot to spill-out
In this world where everyone is super occupied with a
loud shout
Someone to lend me his time and helping me out
That's all I want

16. The Trust

Trust is a feeling
A feeling which establishes a bond
A bond which fabricates love
A love which resonates your life
A life which makes you feel contented
It is all **transitive** in life

Ride it swiftly to the heights
Connect with people on this flight
Try to hold them just with a glimpse of your adorable
sight
Not with your wrist tight
But don't let them to take your journey so light
It is all **reflexive** in life

You love someone blindly implies that you trust them
blindly
You trust someone blindly implies that you love them
blindly

It is all **symmetric** in life

33

Those who are not contented with their life, they have
lack of love.
Those who are not feeling loved, they have lack of
bonding.
Those who don't have any bonding, they have trust
issues.
Try to focus on your trustworthiness, without being a
gullible one.
You are the chauffeur of your life journey, don't let it be
hold by other someone.

First Trust yourself.
Then allow others to trust you.
Have faith in others.
Allow them to have faith in you.

17. The Priority

The bundle of chores, at home, in the workplace and
where you step in,
Never will allow to foster the time in you for someone to
grep in.

The moving traffic around road, rail and river
Maybe will take you to your destination, have they ever
saw your in shiver ?

The fellow colleagues, the team meetings and the
multiple calls
They might guide you to your career goal, will they care
for your loved ones at all?

The early morning games, late night parties and the
random meetups
Surely they give you an adrenalin rush, when did they
overshadow the ones waiting for your single catchup.

It is always about the priority we set, whether its home,

workplace, sports or the dear ones
Everyone has the same bandwidth, 24 hours, whether a
friend, spouse, family or special ones

It is always about what we like the most, whether a good
career, good marks or a nice job
Nothing will come to us free of cost, now it is our choice,
to set the time for the all better knobs

Not saying to prioritise others before you, rather plan
your priority and learn to say NO
If not sure about your choice then never commit and set
yourself as priority for others you know

This is about the life you want in long run, avoid these
small pushbacks for something you wish for,
Plan your, not full day but plan your mind to resonate
with your heart; so you never crave for something,
which was yours

With the small decisions and loose priority check, we
often are on the right side of the biased toss
The time will let you know, what will you profit and
what will be your loss.

It is not a one-day habit, it is life long methodology,
where your need to choose and say YES to those you

belong to,
Prioritising does not take time but only if you have a
heart, mind and soul, to go together all along too.

Learn to prioritise
Follow your heart
Let your heart resonate with your brain
And never ever end-up, because your priority went in
vain

18. The Award Theory

If then, then this
If then, then that
Does this really help in the race we call life?

I see a kid being given chocolate,
only if he recites a poem, without getting late.
I see a student being given a favorite pencil box,
only if he secures good marks, even if it takes an
equinox.
I see the same grown-up kid, buying himself shades of
premium brand,
only if he gets the promotion, even if it takes years to
reach that yard.
And I see the pattern created, imprinted in the brain as a
good scar,
only being awarded for the achievements made so far.

No No No
This was never meant to be the part of the theory of
existence

Survival is not only meant for the ones who rise to every
occasion, with success fence!
Can't we simply give chocolate to a kid and gift to the
student
only because they want?
Just because we are thankful for their existence in our
life!
Rather not for the achievements to boast at certain levels
of life.

Just to make them understand the value of money,
health, and power,
Don't use this barter system and simply raise the
'expectations tower.'
Tell them they are special not only today but every day,
And let them figure out their way out of problems some
or other day.
Guide them, teach them, and impart the facts, illuminate
their minds,
Let them be the best judge for their every finds.

So here's a thought to ponder, as we tread this earthly
shore,
Let kindness be the currency, not rewards for what's in
store.
For life is more than earning, it's a tapestry we weave,

Threads of joy and compassion, in every heart that believes.

19. Thankfulness

Waking up every morning on your comfy bed,
Gazing in the centre of the ceiling fan,
Feeling the sunshine coming from window,
Getting ready for the day,
with the hope of some good for the day
Be thankful, and keep bleak emotion at the bay

Having the food on your plate
Sipping tea, coffee or water at the end
Grabbing the bite and rushing to the work
Buying the frosts, fries and candies from vendors
just to fulfil the desire to please your taste receptors
Be thankful, and be delightful to every stimulus reactors

Living with your loved ones,
Getting a call from your dear ones
Or receiving the messages of good morning/good night
Talking over the phone and connecting over video calls

With the idea of spreading love and sharing life, little
and all
Be thankful, and not be cynical at any connection ball

Carrying the best attire
Wearing the ironed outfit
Or having the accessories to lit more to them
Or simply having clothes to protect you from any tear
With the sense of fashion, attraction or merely action
Be thankful, and never be haughty to show-off in this
section

Having the good eyesight to look around the world
Having a healthy body-mind to take the decision and act
And having resources to keep them fit, treat it as a
blessing
And keep this gift of God fit, hearty and strong
With the gratefulness in heart, aura and soul
Be thankful, and never judge someone from outer sole

20. The Conscience Code

How do we define what's right, what's wrong?
Are ethics fixed, or do they belong
To moments, minds, and shifting ground—
Do they hold firm, or circle round?

No book exists to draw the line,
No written word, no clear design.
What's right for one, may not be so,
For someone else—it might not glow.

Being right won't promise bliss,
Being wrong's not a guaranteed miss.
It's all a lens, a way we see—
A shade of truth for you and me.

It's not moral science we obey,
But what our conscience has to say.
Formed by moments we have known,
Felt, and lived, and made our own.

An answer shaped not from a page,
But thoughts, and nature, and our age.
It won't mislead, it won't betray,
It clears the clutter in your way.

"Honesty is the best policy," they say—
But not for every time or day.
A child may ask, but not yet know,
And truth, too sharp, might steal their glow.

So you decide what must be told,
A softened truth, a heart consoled.
That too is honest, pure, and wise—
Ethics seen through conscious eyes.

To act or not—to hurt or care,
To speak, to hold, to just be fair.
Sometimes selfishness may grow,
Or sometimes it may bring someone low.

Intersection points arrive,
Where choices crash, yet we survive.
Compare the paths, and feel the weight,
Prioritise before too late.

You might be standing all alone,
No echo, light, or guiding tone.

But still, your conscience stands as law—
A compass none can ever flaw.

Don't judge too fast, nor let bias win,
Stay grounded in the truth within.
Before you weigh another's fate,
Know what your heart can tolerate.

Accept your choice, its joy or pain—
Let no regret come back again.
Conscience won't let you down, you'll see—
Be proud of it. And just let it be.
Be proud of it—and fly free.

21. Strength

We fall weak
We become fragile
Expect someone to take us to the next mile

We become untidy
Every ray looks darker
Expect someone to strengthen us even stronger

And we fall again
Expecting the same support again

Try to look at the side
We standing without expectations
Riding our drive on our set of conditions

Yes, there are waves and tides
Be patient and become your guide
Take a look, you are sailing here, in the ocean so wide

Oh, I got up a little
My confidence this time is not so brittle

We work hard
Chasing the dreams which used to hover
Starting a world with our new power

Oh, I finally stood up
My energy is pushing me a level up

Don't look back
Don't bother others hack
It's their problem what they lack

Oh, I am flying
Synergies of my heart and mind unifying

I am Me
Amazing Me
Enthusiastic Me
I love this new me